ARCHWAY's CHRISTMAS NEW YEARS RHYMES

Archie E. Anderson

ARCHWAY'S CHRISTMAS NEW YEARS RHYMES

A Mythbreaker Book

First Edition

© Copyright 2013 Archie Edgar Anderson (1917-) & Donald Murray Anderson (1950-)

All rights reserved. Without limiting rights under copyright reserved above, no part of this book may be reproduced, stored in or introduced into a retrieval system, or transmitted in any form or by any means (electronic, mechanical, photocopying, recording, or otherwise) without prior written permission of the copyright owner.

For information address: mythsbreaker@myway.com

RHYMES

Hazel introducing the rhymes in rhyme

Special Christmas Gift

Christmas Comes

Christmas Double

Memory Christmas

This Christmas

Booty

Christmas Carol Reborn

Christmas Cheer

Christmas Chime

Christmas Early

Christmas Farewell

Christmas Game

Christmas Gifts

Christmas Goodies

Christmas Magic

Christmas Peace and **

Christmas Way

Holy Knight?

Humbug Hope

Magic Misteltoe

New Star

One Christmas Gift

Our Same Trio

Perfect Gift

Santa Cause

Santa Fanta?

Santa Pay-Off

Santa Symbol

Santa Wish

Santa Thawed

Spirit Gone?

Thoughts From Santa

To Boot

Brief Pause

Another

Let's Try Again

New Dose

New Year Pledge

Old New Year

Re-Solved

New

All Year Christmas

Christmas Peace

Christmas Plus

Christmas Plus

Christmas Wish

Christmas Wish

Christmas - - Mark - Plus

New Year's Plus

Perennial Resolution

Christmas Plus

Christmas Plus

Christmas Plus

Our Gift

Everlasting Gift

Christmas-In-Deed

Loving Years

A Year Of Happy Days

Christmas Hope

Christmas And New Year Greetings

Christmas Blessings

A Christmas

Editor's Note:

Yes, some poems have exactly the same titles.

But who would have it otherwise, in a season renowned for hope, wishes, and many pluses?

These poems celebrate 75 Christmases in the life of Archie E. Anderson, so far. As usual Archie's work is comprehensive and thorough, covering every aspect of the season, including the fun, the traditions, the personal, the symbols, the folklore, the legends, etc.

Anyone who loves the finale of every European calendar year will find something to enjoy in this special, holiday, collectors' edition of the <u>Archway</u> series in the <u>Terrian Journals</u> collection.

Archie celebrates the festive season in joyful, humorous, and reflective rhymes, writing for particular people and all of us too.

As usual, Hazel is a prime inspiration and the chief recipient of Archie's work. In this volume, she also responds to Archie in poetry, during the first pages and first of their years sharing life together. Hazel also adds a line to complete Archie's most recent festive poems.

                 - Donald Murray Anderson

Introducing Archway's
Christmas New Years Rhymes

a poem to the poet

by Hazel E. Anderson

Last Christmas eve it is quite true –

I began to write a poem for you;

Believe it or not I was doing fine

Until I reached the ending line.

And then the New Year came along

Now, stop me short if I am wrong

I said that by the end of this year

I would finish the verse and you would cheer.

Sometimes I watch you and I wonder

How you write poems without a blunder

It is an art I quite agree

Done better p'raps by you than me.

If you think my verse is very bad

Just let me know –

I won't feel sad

Remember that in all I do

I always ask for help from you.

Special Christmas Gift

Remember our first Christmas

When world was in a muss;

For gifts we had no money,

But we had a precious us.

Years have swiftly passed along,

And worldly things have come too;

But no gift can ever be

Great as gift of me and you.

Others do great riches have,

But still far from happy life.

The most precious gift we do share

Is our love as man and wife.

Christmas Comes – –

If I should wake on Christmas

Morn to find an empty tree,

It wouldn't matter, honey

While my arms you filled for me

If I should wake on Christmas

Morn to find two stockings slack;

With you by my side, how could

I call such a moment black?

If I should wake on Christmas

Morn and find no gifts around,

I'd be happy to reach out

And know; sweet you could be found

If I should wake on Christmas

Morn without a crumb in sight,

Yet know, hon, that you were near;

Everything would turn out right.

If I should wake on Christmas

Morn, roused gently by your kiss,

Our day could end right there, with

Not a thing for us to miss.

If we should wake on Christmas

Morn, any future day,

We'll be sure to hold us tight − −

And not let us get away

Christmas Double

Christmas, with its gifts and wishes,

Tinsel, lights, and tempting dishes,

Renews the hope that I hold dear

For every moment of each year.

In this stocking hanging season

I possess a perfect reason

For wanting "Claus" to fill up two.

(And neither more nor less will do.)

You have the answer, darling wife;

It makes no difference what the pair

So long as, in them, you are there.

Memory Christmas

This year we have for Christmas

Thoughts of those we've shared;

Of how each one was perfect,

Just because we cared.

Christmas last year led the rest

As with life complete,

For each other gift was us –

Love that can't be beat.

We for now can celebrate

Twenty fifth this year,

Keeping it inside our hearts –

It's, remember, dear.

Though we spend this one apart,

Comfort has these crumbs,

We'll never miss another

When tomorrow comes

This Christmas

Once again that man is here;

This guy shows up every year.

He brings gifts for all, they say --

What cares he who has to pay.

Christmas Spirit is the thing,

Everyone its praises sing.

But take care your "Spirit's" right --

Morning follows every night.

Bells ring out for peace on earth,

And goodwill—but what's it worth;

With Europe's bombs bursting 'round

"Pieces" only can be found.

Everyone has greeting gay,

Saved a year for Christmas Day.

Does it not seem rather queer

Not to spread it through the year?

Booty

This boot is filled with dream stuff,

Especially for you,

To make your Christmas happy,

And spread through New Year too.

Smiling heap of friendly thoughts

For you to share with all;

A dash of understanding,

For humans great and small.

Of course there's Christmas spirit,

Brim full from tip of toe,

With goodwill enough to last,

At least for year or so.

May this boot hold all your hopes

For Christmas and beyond;

May it bulge with happy thoughts,

And dreams, for day undawned.

Tucked inside this Christmas boot

Is much you cannot see;

Wishes for a Christmas Bright,

And ever-sparkling tree.

Christmas Carol Reborn

Days of Scrooge and Cratchit,

Dim relic of our past,

Except for place we know

Where <u>relic</u> seems to last.

When office is too cold,

Thin ghost of Cratchit's there;

Though staff shake and shiver,

Who to complain would dare?

The wrath of Scrooge descends

When anyone is late;

And those who dare be sick

Invite an awful fate.

Those silly laughs must stop,

Must have no joking here;

Happy Humbug Christmas—

Work harder in New Year.

Christmas Cheer

Peace on earth, except, perhaps

A few trouble spots

Where, from day to day, are heard

A few friendly shots.

Peace on earth, if you don't count

Indo China bombs;

Even on the Emerald Isle,

Life is almost calm.

Goodwill to man, well, almost;

Arab oil tents fold

As Israelis' few good friends

Shiver in the cold.

Goodwill to man, everywhere

Energy is shared;

But, of course, for those without,

    Nothing can be spared.

Peace on earth for every man;

    Goodwill may abound

    Although, universally,

    Simply can't be found.

Christmas Chime

Each bell tells a story

In daily life of sound,

From alarm, to door bell

When good friends drop around.

Most peoples' day begins

With jangle of alarm;

And, the bells continue

To signal and to charm.

From telephone to church,

Bells' news is good, or bad;

Can sing of happy times;

The mournful and the sad.

Some bells gently whisper,

Some clang with noisy shout.

Each year, the happy bells

Of Christmas Day ring out.

The song of Christmas bells,

With promise from above,

Rings out hope that someday

World hate will turn to love.

Christmas Early

So glad own Christmas gift you bought;

That lets me off the hook.

Now, when I wander through the stores,

All I need do is look.

You bought your own, now go ahead

And wrap it as you wish;

No need to worry if it's right,

Nor for more gift thoughts fish.

One gift that's bound to satisfy;

If only one you get,

You'll be quite happy Christmas Day;

You'll want no more -- I'll bet!

Christmas Farewell

Here's a Christmas Sampler

From one who aids the Santa Gent.

May you get the spirit;

Joy is the jolly gent's intent.

May this small symbol of

An extra special time of year

Add to wondrous season

You share with those most dear and near.

Have a happy Christmas

And new year filled with perfect days.

Will think of you often

As we all go our separate ways.

Christmas Game

The oldest hippy in the world,

With the long white beard, and suit of red;

With belly-laugh, and shape to match,

Has not the sense to go to bed.

He hitches skinny caribou

(Some people think the name's reindeer.)

To ancient sleigh he overflows;

Does flying saucer bit each year.

This silly gent, despite his years,

Flies 'round world, one night there and back.

Claims he supplies all boys and girls,

From single, bulging, gunny sack.

It is quite clear, this senile gent,

Who lives all year at cold North Pole,

Must have, indeed, a frozen brain,

To play, so long, such far out role.

Not only does he fly, he says,

(He must be conning tiny tots.)

Can squeeze fat form quite quickly down

The smallest, hottest chimney pots.

This old gent, with his midget gang,

Builds many toys, with cheerful will;

No need to worry or to fret;

He knows, the public pays the bill.

Christmas Gifts

It was right before Christmas,

With list in my hand,

Thought I'd soon buy the best things

My budget could stand.

But the first store I entered

Caught me by surprise

As the hordes of wild shoppers

Foiled first dozen tries.

I soon rose to the challenge,

Took vitamin pill;

Hoped my health plan's full coverage

Would pay doctor's bill.

As I neared my objective,

With victory in sight − −

Speaker thanked me for shopping

And wished me good night.

Early next morning arose

With new battle plan;

I'd be very first shopper

(At least the first man.)

When I reached the first counter

With triumphant shout,

Heard the clerk say, a sneering,

"Dear sir, we're sold out!"

Though I was a bit daunted,

Kept plugging along,

Finally bought all the presents

(But, not for a song).

Safe home the car had been left

To save parking fuss;

So with armfuls of parcels,

Pushed on to a bus.

There was standing room only

For me and my bags;

In a moment my parcels

And clothes were in rags.

Finally reached home, worn and wan,

And crept into bed

Where the visions of mob scenes

Danced 'round in my head.

Taking bows and gay ribbons,

And greatest of care,

Completed Christmas wrapping

With minutes to spare.

Can't quite relax as I hope

That all gifts are right,

And not one be discarded

Before Christmas Night.

May the great gift of Christmas

Be yours Christmas Day;

May the spirit True Christmas

Be with you always.

Christmas Goodies

That fat old jolly gent is back,

Grandaddy of the welfare kings;

Will fill most stockings to the top.

Not always what we want, he brings.

Here's sample sweet of what's ahead;

Should help to put you in the mood

To live it up for week or two

With parties, gifts, and much rich food.

No matter how you celebrate

Be sure to follow spirit bright

And spread good will both far and wide

At least full year both day and night.

Christmas Magic

There's magic in this cane
For those who hold the key;
Not easy to explain,
But those who know will see.

When magic cane you wave,
And give a friendly smile,
Your daily path you'll pave
With everything worth while.

While sweet cane's near at hand
There's nothing you should fear;
Just smile and understand,
Good friends are always near.

If Christmas cane is lost,
Eaten up, or broken,
Regardless of the cost,
I'll replace sweet token.

This symbol of good will
(May magic never end)
Is yours to keep until
Last Christmas you attend.

Christmas Peace and **

Every year a child's reborn

Within the hearts of most,

Renewing all the wonder,

As Christmas time we toast.

Every year with hope renewed

We wish all humans well

As peace we pledge, and good will;

Oh happy Christmas spell.

Every year we all should share

Love spirit, every one,

And keep Christmas ever fresh;

May it be never done.

Every year should have its share

Of Christmas cheer each day,

And good will to every one;

Then peace might come to stay.

Christmas Way

Santa is alive and well,

Despite what some may say.

You can count on jolly gent;

His spirit's here to stay.

So long as there is kind deed,

A thankful song to sing,

So long as a friend remains,

Our Christmas bells will ring.

So long as we keep our faith,

There's hope for all mankind;

So long as true spirit's kept,

There's Christmas in each mind.

Christmas can the worst survive,

The worst of strain and strife,

So long as few souls will make

Christmas thoughts way of life.

Holly Knight?

In this season of the holly,

Thought perhaps it would be jolly

To give you branches from our tree,

With berries red for all to see.

I wish I had some mistletoe;

But some one dear would say, "No! No!"

And even if there's some about,

My nerve will probably give out.

Enjoy the holly while you may;

Enjoy a Christmas bright and gay.

When next year comes, you never know,

There just might be some mistletoe.

Humbug hope

Christmas? Humbug? But of course;

Plus at least a score or so

Of other things, bad or worse,

That you may not want to know.

Hidden commercial mess,

Faint flame flickers now and then

As hope springs each year anew;

Good will to Ms and to men.

Christmas could be great success,

Spirit spread throughout the year,

If everyone, every day,

Would share a smile, hung with cheer.

Magic Mistletoe

Sweet magic of the mistletoe

Is yours, no matter where;

Results are always guaranteed,

Waved over head in air.

Each berry means a single kiss,

Legend says, one alone;

You pluck a berry after kiss- -

With nil, you're on your own.

If these instructions aren't too clear,

Here's what I'll gladly do;

Bring armful huge of mistletoe,

And demonstrate for you.

This artificial mistletoe

Has charm that cannot miss;

But don't be disappointed if

You get a plastic kiss.

New Star

Two thousand weary years

Since Christmas Star shone bright;

Now history's gloom is lit

By beacon of the night.

Kohoutek, promise brings,

Or is it just false hope,

Which merely flares, and dies;

Leaves world in dark to grope.

Some think it an omen,

A chance to gain fresh start;

Others fear may be doom,

And wonder's in each heart.

Visit by Kohoutek

May more than light our skies,

Reminding all who watch

Where earth's real power lies.

May this be a symbol

Of second chance for world;

New dawn for human kind;

Good will, and peace, unfurled.

One Christmas Gift

Each Christmas is the same

Yet always fresh and new;

How could it ever change

So long as I'm with you.

Upon this Christmas day,

As we have done each year,

Enjoyment's not just gifts

But something far more dear.

Christmas is forever;

Each day throughout each year

We have true gift of love,

The dearest of the dear.

Our Same Trio

It was half a million dreams ago

Life and Christmas gained a special glow;

One which started with such lack of fuss,

Very few our gifts; but we had us.

Each year we gained memories by the score,

Yet, there will be always room for more.

Our love-light will be always room for more.

Until the end – no regrets, no tears.

Perfect Gift

Every year, the Christmas gifts

For you, from me, are spread

Underneath the Christmas tree;

Buy only few, you said.

You'd be happy with one gift,

But always give you more;

And, when shopping time runs out,

Could buy another score.

If gave million gifts or so,

Plus extra two or three,

They never could quite equal

Your gift of love for me.

Santa Cause

People do odd things

It seems, for kick;

Strangest one of all,

Fat guy, Saint Nick.

Some high flier he;

Despite his age,

Over roof tops climbs,

With love, not rage.

He takes great delight

Unloading pack;

Once he squeezes down

Each chimney stack.

Should stay home at night

But then, could be

Simply cannot stand

North Pole T.V.

This obese wee gent

Does spread good cheer;

Why not indulge him,

Once every year.

Santa Fanta?

Alas, poor Santa Claus

Is really in a stew.

Now it seems, inflation,

Has finally caught him too.

Gone are the happy days

When all good girls and boys

So often were quite pleased

With simple games and toys.

Before the mini-skirt,

The whiskered gent could cope,

But now there's been a blow

To quickly dash last hope.

If he has the gifts for all,

Now how do you suppose

He'll find the time to stuff

Two billion panty-hose?

This may be bad, but still,

What can be more shocking

Is Christmas Eve child hangs

Full length body stocking.

Santa Pay-Off

Prices going up,
Values going down,
And to add to lead,
Santa comes to town.

Fat, inflated one
Promises to all
Anything they want;
Simply write or call.

Pudgy, rotund one
Is a well-liked chap;
He gets all the cheers,
Girls climb on his lap.

He smiles cheerfully
As the socks he fills;
Ho, ho, ho, he laugh – –
We, not him, pay bills.

Santa Symbol

Here's sweet, jolly Santa

With greetings of great cheer,

Bringing you best wishes

For Christmas and all year.

Now lucky are the ones

Who trust this bearded gent,

And know he is for real − −

They know his real intent.

If good old Santa Claus

Means something real to you,

You'll find you always can

Make special dreams come true.

True belief in Santa

Makes world a better place,

If you practise daily,

And all life's truth can face.

May you truly savour

Fat Santa, sweet and small,

And find Christmas spirit

Within your heart, for all.

Santa Wish

Here's special treat from Santa;

Small, sweet Christmas gift,

Designed to make you chuckle,

Give your spirit lift.

Hope your Christmas, and beyond,

Shines with joy and light;

Hope for you, the brand new year

Dawns on future bright.

May your happy Christmas have

Blessings from above;

May the gifts you give and get

Have true glow of love.

Snow Thawed

For all the true snow lovers

Let's shed a silent tear

For all that gorgeous white stuff

That is no longer here.

Too bad something can't be done

To make their Christmas white,

With tons of fluffy light stuff

To make their Yuletide bright.

For all persistent snow birds,

Deep freeze is very thing;

Put them there with heaps of snow,

And thaw them out next spring.

Spirit gone?

Santa helper stop,

Retire from the race?

After all, it is

A choice that all must face.

When this helper goes

Who'll aid Saint Valentine

With his sweetheart sweets

And pen poetic line?

Easter Bunny, too,

May feel a bit bereft

As soon as he knows

Egg-handling friend has left.

May this Christmas be

A happy joyful one,

And may all your days

Be filled with love and fun.

This is not the end,

Even though you fear it.

Special days each year,

Will be here in spirit.

Thoughts from Santa

Santa Season's here again;

Gifts are order of the day.

Makes no matter, large or small,

It's thought that counts, so they say.

Here's small sample in advance

From one who helps jolly gent;

Hope it is beginning of

Happy holiday well spent.

No expense was spared to bring

This preview of festive fare.

Christmas gift you see is small;

Thought expands for all to share.

To Boot

On behalf of Santa,

Would like to give you boot;

You will no doubt get kick

When you examine loot.

The goodies big and small

Were all hand-picked for you.

Hope they give you pleasure,

And give a few laugh, too.

Santa won't go barefoot;

(That's just in case you care.)

He can depend on elves

To make another pair.

About old Santa's feet;

You may think boots too small,

Until you think he must

Down tiny chimneys crawl.

Brief Pause

Birthday of the new year

Most people celebrate;

They write new plans and hopes

Upon a brand-new slate.

Some hope to start afresh,

Get rid of habits bad,

Enjoy a happy year

Without a moment sad.

Spirit keeps on glowing,

One week, or maybe two,

Then everyone slips back;

Old thoughts, bad habits too.

Another

Another chance,

Another year;

Another step,

Another fear.

Another try,

Another show;

Another stop,

Another go.

Another war,

Another peace,

Another start,

Another cease.

Another death,

Another birth;

Another bomb,

Another earth.

Let's Try Again

On threshold of another year,

We look ahead with hope and fear;

In these uncertain times, we know,

There is a better way to go.

No matter how we carefully plan,

There really is no way we can

Tell what new year will mean to all;

Disasters great or blessings small.

Some wise predictions do come true;

We'll know for sure when year is through.

But, no one ever hopes for less

Than prosperous year, plus happiness.

New Dose

May you have a great New Year

Nineteen hundred, seven five.

Most will feel they are in luck

If full year they stay alive.

Resolutions may be fine,

If some good ones can be found;

But, looking at year gone by,

Hope this time we don't lose ground.

This year, for sure we'll cure

Our world of all its ills,

Have peace for evermore,

While we keep taking pills.

New Year Pledge

Started out afresh

Happy New Year's day;

This time won't slip back

From new better way.

Made imposing list,

Resolutions good;

Set my sights quite high

As resolvers should.

Covered every point,

Faults and habits bad

Resolved to reform,

Make my critics sad.

Haven't yet begun

To adopt new plan;

Will get underway

Quickly as I can.

Will start better life,

Find good things I seek,

Tomorrow, maybe;

But, for sure, next week.

Old New Year

Seconds of our lives trickle down

To add to heap, one more dead year.

Each tiny grain of time is spent;

Paid for by smile, or frown, or tear.

This is no time to sit and moan

So little worthwhile has been done.

Look up and look ahead to see

How best to use new year begun.,

When you consider your small part,

Look ahead with hope, not despair.

Future of our world, after all,

Is one plus one, plus one affair.

Re-solved

No matter if the old ones

Lie broken, scattered, torn;

In the debris something stirs

As hope anew is born.

Though new ones may be added,

Most take the tattered bits,

Patch them up as best they can,

And hope the patched one fits.

To avoid the stress and strain,

There is sure solution;

Just resolve you'll never make

New Year's Resolution.

New

New Year

New Deeds

New Debts

New Weeds

New Hopes

New Tears

New Laughs

New Fears

New Chance

New Ties

New Truths

New Lies

New Age

New Youth

New Thoughts

New Proof

New Night

New Day

New View

New Way

New Style

New Clothes

New Star

New Pose

New Spring

New Fall

New Ditch

New Wall

New Crime

New Cure

New Dirt

New Pure

New Start

New End

New Twist

New Bend

New Guess

New Doubt

New In

New Out

New Fast

New Slow

New Stay

New Go

New Speed

New Rate

New Luck

New Fate

New Skip

New Jump

New Dip

New Hump

New Far

New Near

New Squint

New Peer

New Date

New Time

New Words

New Rhyme

New Grapes

New Wines

New Frown

New Lines

New Kings

New Queens

New Show

New Scenes

New Pain

New Fun

New Year

Soon Done.

All Year Christmas

Yes, it is that time again;

One more Christmas that we share.

But, we celebrate all year;

Day by day we show we care.

Many people seem to have

Christmas spirit for one day;

But we both know it lives on,

In our hearts, in every way.

We have that certain something

That comes from years of sharing.

Christmas is just one more day

To share our love and caring.

Christmas Peace

Mistletoe and holly are

Expression of festive time.

Red and white and green, they bring

Rich Christmas gift so sublime.

Year after year we should find

Christmas old and ever new

Has a magic all may share,

Regardless of daily view.

It is season of delight

So full of peace and of love;

Too bad its time is so brief.

May sun of peace shine above,

And all people of this earth

Share the peace that comes from dove.

Christmas Plus

Christmas is time for fun,

The time for smiles and for love;

The time to pledge from the heart

And petty strife rise above.

Now and in the future days,

On and on from year to year,

We'll share our love at Christmas

And each day throughout the year.

May spirit true of Christmas,

Through each day of year, endure.

But, whatever lies ahead,

Our love is for certain sure.

Christmas Plus

There was a special, precious gift

On Christmas ninety-five.

Had most delightful present when

You really did arrive.

Oh such a vision to behold,

With sparkling eyes of blue

And smile that was so full of love,

That comes to me from you.

Charming sweetheart you are indeed;

Will always hold you dear.

You bring love and happy sunshine

Whenever you appear.

Enjoyed your visit, short and sweet.

Too soon we had to part.

Will always keep the memory of

Your wave, from heart to heart.

Christmas Wish

Make a Christmas wish,

And may it come true.

Really hope you make

It a good one, too.

Always wish for you,

Near and dear to me,

Never ending love;

Ever may it be.

Christmas Wish

May Christmas be a happy time

As friends and family gather 'round;

Re-affirming their affection

In thought and deed and joyous sound.

All good wishes come from the heart.

Now and each moment through new year

Nice thoughts of you will always flow.

Every you will be sweetheart dear.

Christmas –Mark– Plus

Most Christmas gifts are well received;

A few are simply put away.

Hope this item is a special one,

To use and enjoy every day.

Whatever you may choose to read,

May it give double pleasure.

Enjoyment of the printed word,

And a book mark you can treasure.

Day or night, anything you read,

When you pause part way through a book,

Be sure, with care, to mark your place,

And you'll know, next time, where to look.

Day By Day

When you sit, disconsolate,

Amid mess of holiday debris,

There is no single surprise left,

Under shredded Christmas tree.

Somehow survived the Christmas rush;

Boxing Day was not hard to take;

While New Year's day did bring new hope,

Did resolutions too soon break.

It would seem, best plan is,

Meet each day with friendly smile;

Face the bad, enjoy the good;

Make all days you live, worthwhile.

New Year's Plus

New Year's Day, tradition has,

Time to resolve and renew.

Resolutions often fade

Quickly in a month or two.

When one resolves from the heart,

Good intentions do persist;

Benefits for near and dear

From such resolution list

Here's resolve for every day

Throughout this and every year

Will cherish you, near or far,

As sweet, extra-special dear.

Perennial Resolution

As some sit and sadly ponder,
Amid embers of dying year,
And their broken resolutions,
A spark of hope does soon appear.

A few sit and bemoan the past,
Although there's no way to change it.
All can look forward to New Year;
At any age, all can share it.

As for New Year's Resolutions;
A good one all of us can share:
Always do your best every day,
And show loved ones how much you care.

Christmas Plus

Christmas is a memory time,

When we reminisce about

The years we've been together,

Some with our future in doubt.

To keep the Christmas spirit

Is our aim throughout the year;

Ever hoping those we meet

Will respond from far and near.

So, here's to us at Christmas,

And the love we'll always share;

As we know, within our hearts,

Each day shows how much we care.

Christmas – Plus

As we add another Christmas,

We go through our memory file

Since our first love set in tennis,

Have added memories, smile by smile.

As we continue on in life,

We know each Christmas time we share,

Our love will stay strong through the year,

And, daily show, how much we care.

Christmas Plus

Christmas comes again;

Make it fifty plus

Since the happy day

Love first came to us.

Could it really be,

Oh so long ago,

We had only us,

And no more to show?

Though we have come far

Up the scale, it seems

We are just the same

As at start of dreams.

Christmas times we share

Spirit and great life

That we've always had;

Loving man and wife.

Everlasting Gift

Of all the gifts at Christmas,

The one we share is the best.

Through many years together,

It has always stood the test.

We do share the gift of love;

Of that, there can be no doubt.

A gift we both will have,

Every day, the year throughout.

Our Gift

About ten thousand dreams ago,

First Christmas we did share.

Each time we add another one

We show how much we care.

As for gifts, there have been many;

All sizes, big and small,

But one repeats, year after year,

And it still leads them all.

There is no equal to the one

That always ranks above;

The precious gift we give to us;

The one we share − − our love.

Christmas – In – Deed

Here's to us, another Christmas,

A time of giving we two share

We know it takes more than mere gifts

To show how much we really care.

Day after day we make our way,

Facing whatever life may bring.

No matter whether good or bad,

Together we have everything.

Though presents are nice to receive

There's something that rates far above.

No matter what the future holds,

We'll always share the gift of love.

Loving Years

Another year, at Christmas time:

Another year to celebrate:

Another year for memories:

Another year for happy date.

Another year add to our score:

Another year will soon be due:

Another year with extra day:

Another year of love for you.

A Year Of Happy Days

Happiness is most pleasant theme,

As we, fresh start do seek again;

Putting aside, for the moment,

Past disappointments and past pain.

You should look upon the bright side:

No sense dwelling on the past:

Enjoy life; let smiles be your guide.

What lies ahead, we can't forecast.

You should cherish every friendship.

Each one has something they can give.

Always concentrate on today;

Remember, this is the day we live.

Christmas Hope

Christmas time love and happiness,

Is precious gift we always share.

We add to our sweet memories

And daily show how much we care.

Though Christmas Day we celebrate;

Each and every day of the year,

We know, when we awake each morn,

We renew love we hold so dear.

Christmas & New Year Greetings

Happy celebration,

No matter where you be.

This wondrous day each year,

Is best, we should agree.

Also, there's New Years Day,

Which offers a new start,

As we greet all our friends.

With wishes from the heart.

No matter what your faith,

We should look up, not down.

One smile is worth far more

Than the most ugly frown.

Christmas Blessings

At this time of year,

May all have a happy time.

Enjoying every moment,

Recalling music,

Remembering rhyme.

You share with many others,

Cheerful night and day spent.

Hope that you will always find,

Royal Blessing is for all,

In both your heart and mind.

Show others how much you care,

There's always room for a smile.

May we ever be aware,

As we greet many others,

Saying Christmas is everywhere.

A Christmas

Another Christmas for all of us to share

Can have special greeting for everyone

Happy moments, as we show we do care

Remember celebrating we have done.

It's well worth every blessing day and night

Sunshine or snowdrops, wherever you are*

To all your friends, no matter near, or far

May they have great memories to share,

As they enjoy most happy times,

Sharing past and more present everywhere.

(* Line by Hazel E. Anderson)

**Other writings in the
Terrian Journals collection:**

A Sketch of Terrian History

Terrian Journals: Living as a Newcomer

Middle Earth Journals

Rediscovery Journals

Fukurokuju No Kasumi Journals

Sabbatical Journals

Departure Journals

Adventuredate Unknown

Terrian Journals NSR Not Spying, … Really!

Terrian Journals' JNG Jokes Nobody Gets

Terrian Journals for the Misguided

Terrian Journals First Anthology

Terrian Journals Second Anthology

Archway: Six Year Book Of Dreams

Archway: Lifetime Rhyme

www.ingramcontent.com/pod-product-compliance
Lightning Source LLC
Chambersburg PA
CBHW061337040426
42444CB00011B/2961